Letters of Apology

*How to Stop Waiting for Permission to
Be the Wonderful Person You Are*

Valerie A. Utton MS.Ed.

Letters of Apology
Copyright © 2007 by Valerie Utton.

Published 2011 by Inkwell Productions
Second edition

ISBN 978-0-578-08836-5

CRUCKRUCKRUCKRUCKRUCKRUCKRU

This book is dedicated to my mom, Jackie and my sister, Nancy.

It's one thing to believe in your own dreams. It's quite another to have the people closest to you believe in them too.

To both of you, without your ideas, interest, kind comments and endless rereading this book would not exist. Thank you.

CRUCKRUCKRUCKRUCKRUCKRUCKRU

"The greatest achievement was at first and for a time a dream. The oak sleeps in the acorn, the bird waits in the egg, and in the highest vision of the soul a waking angel stirs. Dreams are the seedlings of realities."

Robert Allen

Preface

Our life begins with dreams. Before we can speak one word, we are able to dream. As we grow up though, we begin to realize there is a difference between sleeping dreams and waking dreams.

If achieving our waking dreams required nothing more than our solitary mental and physical efforts then success would be an everyday occurrence.

It would be the result of plotting a course in the direction of our dreams and successfully engaging and accomplishing each task along the way.

As we all know though, turning our dreams into reality just doesn't feel that simple. But why? We can all dream; why does it feel like successfully turning our dreams into reality is reserved for a privileged few?

It's all those *other* people that have the ability to dream their dreams, plot their course and ultimately succeed in improving the quality of their lives and the lives of the people around them.

Maybe the answer to the question is simpler than we think. Maybe we just haven't given ourselves permission to succeed.

Maybe we keep waiting for a sign from God, the universe, Mom or Dad, whomever or whatever. We're waiting for someone or something *outside* of us to give us permission to believe in the quality of the person and the dreams *inside* of us.

"Nothing out there will ever satisfy you except temporarily and superficially, but you may need to experience many disappointments before you realize that truth"

Eckert Tolle

The thing is we don't realize we're waiting for permission. We just wish the people in our lives would apologize for the things they've said and done to us. If they did, then we'd have the validation we've been looking for so we can believe we are worthy of success or happiness or joy or whatever experience it is that the individual within us dreams of.

The truth is we don't need it. The idea that anyone can give us permission to believe in our own true innate self worth is nothing more than an illusion that can be exposed as easily as we can expose the magic of pulling a coin out of a child's ear.

And just to be clear…you have permission to pursue and achieve your dreams.

Table of Contents

Introduction

I'm SORRY for what I did THis will definetly never never ever ever

HAPPEN AGAIN

sincerely,

I.

Introduction

This is a book full of potential. It's also full of letters; each one written and contributed by a different person. I can't tell you anything about the people who wrote the letters because I don't know anything about them. Not whether they are male or female, how old they are or where they're from because every letter in this book is anonymous.

What I can tell you is that when they heard about this book, they understood what it might mean to someone reading it and made the decision to write and contribute their own letter of apology.

For a few people though, the idea of writing a letter of apology wasn't a possibility and instead of writing a letter of apology, they wrote letters asking for an apology. Two of these letters are included in this introduction as evidence of how profound the lack of an apology can be.

   With these letters as well as all the letters throughout the book there is a temptation to get drawn into trying to understand the complicated lives involved.

   We could veer off the path of this book and take all the psychology we know and use it to try and determine what happened, or to figure out exactly who did what to whom. But in the end all the letters offered here are about the same thing - an apology; nothing more, nothing less, just a simple apology.

   Another temptation is to be sad because these letters are evidence of the things, sometimes not very nice things, people do to each other. But these letters also represent hope and potential.

   They give us every reason to believe that anyone is capable of sincerely regretting the hurt or harm they've caused. When we accept this truth as expressed and shared by all these different people, that's when healing begins.

****

Dear _____,

Do you realize the hurt and pain you have put me through? To this day you have not said you are sorry. It has been years and I try to forgive you but the pain keeps coming back no matter how hard I try to put it in the past.

I have waited for you to apologize to me and acknowledge that you have caused me pain and that you were wrong for what you did and that there are no excuses for your wrong doing.

I have forgiven you and that has helped me find my peace but your apology will complete this situation and put it to rest for good.

Me

****

I believe I am owed an apology because when I was a young teenager my mom thought I was ready to get married to a religious, church-going man 8 years older than me.

After we got married he stopped going to church, started drinking alcohol and physically and mentally abused me. I always thought it was my fault so I kept it to myself for 11 years. When I was living with my mom she never had to hit me or discipline me. But there I was getting abused by a so called religious man.

When my mom finally found out what was happening in my marriage she cried and said "I never had to hit you and here is this man I agreed for you to marry doing it."

I finally left and never, ever looked back. It affected my kids. My teen years were taken away. I feel that my mom let me go too soon and didn't think enough about my future or who this man truly was. He finally accepted who he was and after 15 years he apologized and asked me to forgive him.

I feel my mom owes me an apology for not letting me grow up and find myself and become a real true woman first. I forgave him in order to move on.

A lot of changes have happened in my life. My kids remember but we all learned to forgive and forget. She owes me an apology for making this choice!

1.

Nothing New Under the Sun

Our planet is home to over 6,750,000,000 people. That's a staggering number of living, breathing human beings. Can you imagine how much bigger that number becomes if we include all the people who've populated the planet throughout the centuries?

Yet here we are, standing in the midst of millions trying to do something every other human being that has ever lived has tried to do: define, express and maintain our own unique sense of self.

What's interesting is that even though we share the quest to understand our lives, we spend a lot of our time focusing on the differences between us to come up with the answers.

We think as individuals, act as individuals and maintain our individual, personal space. We hold onto our uniqueness thinking that when we are accepted with all our unique characteristics, beliefs, histories and ideas intact, we have been accepted for who we are.

But then when we look at the people who we've accepted and who've accepted us, we realize it's not based on our differences, it's based on the things we have in common with each other.

We become a part of each other's lives to share things and to support one another. And when we become part of each other's lives we fulfill two of our most basic human needs: to belong and to be loved. The differences between us may help us recognize the face in the mirror, but it's the comfort and security of the things we share that give us the courage to express our individuality.

What this means is that even though we use different methods to get what we want in life, our actions are very often motivated by similar if not the exact same goals. Realizing that we have this in common encourages us to wonder what else we might have in common.

Maybe the things we feel, think, wonder and worry about in our own life are similar or the same as the things other people feel, think, wonder and worry about in their own life; even if that person lived over 500 years ago.

When good fortune comes our way we want to share it with our family and friends because we feel better about ourselves when our actions make the people around us happy.

But when we do things we regret, or bad things happen to us, we tend to look away and hope no one else notices because we're embarrassed. The fact that many of our problems involve the people we count on for the security of knowing we belong and are loved doesn't help.

Instead, we end up trying to understand and deal with our mistakes or misfortunes privately and very often without resolution.

This is a lonely place to be and it's hard to heal when you feel like you're all alone. There's no one there to tell you it's all going to be okay; no one to help you figure out what went wrong, how to fix things or to help you move on.

Some people seek professional help; many more just struggle with thoughts and feelings they're unsure of how to resolve. The more we struggle, the more the distance between us increases.

In these letters, people tell us about the different kinds of mistakes they've made and express their honest and sincere regret for having made them. Reading them encourages us to remember that people – maybe even millions of people – have made similar if not the exact same mistakes.

They also let us know that other people – maybe even millions - have struggled because of someone else's mistakes.

The people who wrote these letters did so by choice. No one stood over them or forced them to write or told them what to write. They were ready to apologize; ready to do what they could to decrease the distance between themselves and the people they hurt.

But these writers did more than that, they left out the names, locations and dates that could have identified who the letter was written for so that we might all find ourselves and finally hear the words we've been hoping to hear.

This is an amazing gift. When we accept it, we accept the truth implied within: that the people who hurt us may feel the same sincere regret for what they did even if they've never spoken or written the words we've longed to hear.

****

To my Fiancé,

From the bottom of my heart I apologize to you for not being faithful to you and messing up our relationship. I totally accept that I was wrong in doing this and I should have never done this to you because you are a good man who didn't deserve it. I was going through a very emotional and confusing stage in my life. I was afraid that the life we had wasn't going to last forever or that we would never make it to where we are now, thinking about getting married.

I truly apologize that I did this to you. I know how much this messed you up emotionally as well as mentally. This also taught me how to be a better and more truthful person to you and

to myself. I have truly accepted that it was my mistake and apologize for it from the bottom of my heart.
Loving you more than ever before,
Me

****

Dear Victims,

Victims all around the world who have been hurt by rape, murder, molestation, robbery, identity theft, assault, stabbings, shootings, discrimination, hate crimes, kidnapping and sadly the list goes on. I wish nothing more than to give everyone of you a hug and an apology. I know you all need one because I am also a victim. I wish each and every day that the men who raped me are put behind bars. It is to the point that now all I want is a simple apology, but I know I will never get that.

Parents, siblings and all people in general, whether you are family of a victim, or even if you know someone who is a victim, I feel sorry for you. Many crimes end with death or kidnapping. I feel remorse for you because you cannot hug that person or tell them you love them. It breaks my heart to know that your loved ones are missing. It makes me appreciate life so much more. I wish that somehow I could help you through your troubles.

I beat myself up every day, because I made a huge mistake. I wish I could take it back, but I can't. With that being said I send my apologies out to victims of robberies. I feel horrible because I robbed an innocent woman. I was with one of my friends and I drank too much liquor. I made a horrible decision. I wish she'd known I would not hurt a fly. I started to walk away and I immediately wanted to give what I took back, but she took out a phone and called the police. Now I am in jail.

If you are reading this you need to know that I am so sorry and I would not have done anything like that if I had been sober. I am also a victim of rape. When I was 15 years old I ran away to the house of a man I trusted. When I got there we started drinking and smoking. Then he called some people over and the next thing I knew I was being held down and my clothes were being pulled off. Then afterwards he kicked me out.

I am not the same because of that. I wonder each and every day why those men did that to me. Now I sometimes have flashbacks and see it happening to me all over again; the screaming, the crying, the fighting, the blood and then to be kicked out into the street like I was trash.

Not only did I commit a horrible crime, but I was the victim of a horrible crime too. As a victim I sometimes feel scared; certain smells set off triggers and make me tense and anxious and sick to my stomach. I can say that

I don't relate to victims of robberies, but I am a victim too so I can understand how a victim must feel to a certain extent. In conclusion, I am very and sincerely sorry to all victims of the world.

Sincerely Yours,

A Regretful Victim

2.

You Have the Right to Remain Silent...

Apologies can be a challenge if we are unaware of the distinction between a confession and an apology. A confession can sound like an apology, but it's not.

A confession is when somebody acknowledges that their actions broke a law, a rule or a code of conduct. Confessions focus on the act rather than on the impact of the results. When people confess they say things like 'Yes, I did it.'

An apology can sound like a confession, but apologies focus on results and the impact those results may have had on a person, place or thing. They acknowledge one person's right to have had a different, usually negative experience as a result of what someone else did.

When people confuse a confession with an apology they are confusing a limited number of laws and rules people can break with an unlimited combination of ways people can legally and socially hurt or harm each other.

Breaking the law is often a black or white issue because either someone broke the law or they didn't. On the other hand, causing hurt or harm as the result of something someone did can be a very gray area even when both sides are aware of what happened.

Sometimes we get a confession, sometimes we get an apology, sometimes we get both and sometimes we get neither.

However the situation unfolds it's after the fact when someone becomes aware of the damage they've done that they come face to face with the uncomfortable dilemma of whether or not to apologize.

It's after the fact for us too because the damage is done and waiting for an apology or some type of acknowledgement of what happened can be just as uncomfortable for us.

We could choose to confront the problem and the person face to face to get the apology, but an apology that's offered after we've brought a situation to someone's attention is hard to decipher. Instead we rationalize that they created the problem so they should make the first move.

We wait for them because we want to know, sometimes need to know, that we matter enough to the other person for them to realize the negative impact their actions have had on us. If they come up with the apology we want to hear on their own it's easier for us to believe they really do regret any hurt or harm we experienced as a result of their action.

What's important to remember with all the gray areas is that people tend to do things because they've gotten caught up with what's going on in their own heads or in the drama of their life. Their goals take center stage and if by choice or chance we're in the way, there's a chance we're going to get bumped and bruised by their actions.

Knowing the difference between a confession and an apology doesn't guarantee we will get either one from anyone. What it does do is help us get clear about what it is we want to hear. And, at the very least, it gives us something to think about while we wait.

****

Dear Son,

      The life that I have lived has not been one of privilege, and is no excuse for not being in your life. I regret that I have allowed you to grow up with only one parent. I am sorry for allowing this jail life to come between you and me, and being there for you when you needed a father. There is nothing I can do to make up for the years I have left you without a father.

      I do believe that you have the right to despise me and the awful mistakes that I have made. It is not the killing or drug crimes I regret, that is the life I chose. The crime of allowing a young man to grow up without a father is the crime I now serve the rest of my life in prison for. The only crime I shed tears for everyday of my shameful life.

      I sincerely write this letter in hope of putting you at peace with the demons I have allowed to fill your soul. I know I have not been there to teach you right from wrong. I hope I have influenced and set enough of an example for you to be nothing like me. If I have done that then I know you will live a long life filled with hope, love, and the motivation to achieve greatness.

I have always loved you,
From the Dad to a stranger

****

Dear Daughter,

I am writing you this letter to say I am sorry for what I did to you when you were a teenager. I didn't know the pain I caused you then would change the direction of your life forever. You didn't do anything to deserve what I did to you. I know that you trusted me as your father to protect you from others. I didn't understand when I molested you that the impact would be so very negative. You did nothing to deserve my actions towards you.

I always wanted to say I was sorry but I didn't know how you would react. You are my firstborn child and I do love you. I wish I could take it back but as you know I cannot. I wish I would have told you this before, but again, as you know, I didn't. You are my daughter and I love you. You are a strong, patient and loving person; you did not deserve what I did, you did nothing wrong. Stay strong and know that from the bottom of my heart I am truly sorry for what I did to you.

Your Father

3.

Seven Magic Words

Apologies feel powerful. An apology can clear the air, mend fences and refresh attitudes. Sometimes though, the apology we get is tough to accept because it includes a litany of justifications or way too much finger pointing. And if it's the third, fifth or umpteenth time we've heard the words it's even harder for us to believe in their sincerity.

The simple fact is that an apology only needs to be seven words long: *I'm sorry I did this to you*. It's all the other words people include that can dilute an apologies ability to resolve a situation.

People shy away from the simplicity of this apology because it's humbling. When delivered with sincerity there's no place to hide, no excuses, nothing, just the simplest of statements that acknowledges and exposes our imperfections in front of another human being.

It's easy to understand why we might avoid or 'forget' that we've done something we should apologize for; it's embarrassing. Nobody likes feeling this kind of vulnerability and yet we all do things we should apologize for.

For most of us it's the small mistakes we neglect to resolve; the little things we would take back in a heartbeat if we could. The wrong words, a simple miscommunication, doing something before thinking it through; we do these things everyday and so does everyone else.

Sometimes people do a good job with the "I'm sorry" part, but without the other five words, how does the listener know what someone is saying they're sorry for?

The person speaking could just as easily be finishing the sentence in their mind with a slew of words that have nothing to do with a sincere apology. Instinctively, we know this.

The "…I did this…" part will let both of us know that we are on the same page talking about the same thing. And if we can agree on what happened, then we should be able to resolve the situation. But it's the last two words, the "…to you" that seal the deal.

When someone finishes their apology with the "…to you" words, it's like a breath of fresh air to us because now we can put the whole situation behind us.

Without the last two words even the simplest, smallest, stupidest issues can take up residency in dark corners of our mind where they threaten to influence all future interactions with that person. If an unresolved issue persists long enough or is severe enough, it has the potential of influencing the way we interact with everyone and everything else in our world.

Human beings interact with each other; that's what we do. No one is perfect and it's impossible for any of us to go through life without occasionally stepping on a few toes.

When our toes are stepped on the desire for an apology can spring to life without any encouragement at all. Just as instinctively we can come up with an idea of what we want to hear. It may not be that easy for the person doing the stepping.   Without some type of knowledge, education or experience even the simplest, most basic stripped down apology can be a challenge.

****

Dear Girlfriend,

First of all, I'm going to start off by saying I am sorry. The reason I am apologizing is because I have been hard on you these last couple of months. I have neglected you in various types of ways. Sorry cannot define how bad I feel.

I love you with all my heart. Losing you in my life would be a total breakdown. I need you now, more than I ever felt I needed you. I know I left our relationship abruptly, and did not explain why or in what direction I was heading. I was testing the waters to see what else was out there. I know my actions set us back, but my love is still here. You were there for me and I was there for you during thick and thin, and under all circumstances. I let my pride get in the way and I let our relationship fall apart. I have grown a lot in the last couple of months and lately I have been feeling regret. I am sincerely sorry and I want you to know that I mean every word I say.

I don't know what the future holds, but I hope it includes some type of relationship with you. Even if our relationship is not intimate, I want to be a part of your life somehow. I love you as a person and more, and I will not let anything get between us again.

Love
Your Boyfriend

****

Dear Wife,

I am sorry for all the pain that I've caused you. I never meant to hurt you. I didn't know how a man was supposed to treat his wife. I didn't understand that I should have cherished and loved you sincerely and with all of my heart. I regret cheating on you, hitting you, neglecting you and running away from my responsibilities as a husband.

I never want to hurt anyone this way again. I realize now what a beautiful, loving and caring person you are. I hope you find love, peace and happiness because I took all of that away from you. I never befriended you and hope that you will find friendship in your next relationship; someone you can talk to, someone who will listen to you and understand and respect your feelings.

I will love you always

I am forever sorry

Your Husband

4.

Teach Your Children Well

Do you remember the first time you had to apologize to someone? How old were you? Did someone coach you on how to do it? Did someone explain to you why it's important to apologize sometimes; or how to recognize when it's appropriate to apologize?

If even one person took the time to give you the inside scoop on how or when you should apologize, you're the exception.

With the best of intentions parents, teachers and role models focus on teaching children behaviors that will direct them away from saying or doing things they end up needing to apologize for.

If a child strays beyond the limits of these predetermined, legally and socially acceptable behaviors, an adult will usually step in to encourage, prod or sometimes force the child to apologize.

But how often do children see their parents, teachers and role models apologize? Rarely, if at all. Our children are much more likely to witness the rise of the problem than they are to witness its resolution.

Instead, without knowing what may have taken place behind closed doors, the creative mind of a child will draw its own conclusion. To their eyes it often appears as if tensions between 'grown-ups' magically disappear.

Is it fair to assume our children will grow up knowing how and when to apologize without witnessing the adults in their world apologizing once in a while? Maybe these children grow up thinking that once you're past a certain age apologies are unnecessary because the problems just disappear.

Is it fair to assume that adults who never apologize do so purely by choice? Maybe adults who never apologize honestly believe problems will go away on their own because that's what they witnessed growing up. Or maybe they just never learned how to apologize.

We try to teach our children the lessons they will need to live a happy and successful life. We don't deliberately neglect passing on the knowledge of knowing how and when to say "I'm sorry I did this to you." We just forget that everything is new to a child and that they will absorb all the lessons we teach them regardless of whether we teach them with intent and purpose or simply imply them with repeated examples.

It's up to us to remember that children watch us interact with each other all the time. If we don't teach our children how and when to say the seven magic words or at the very least lead by example, who will?

****

Dear Daughter,

Let me start by saying that the day you were born was the happiest day of my life. I was so young, barely a teenager and so inexperienced. But when I saw your beautiful face it made the pain go away.

I know you think that you were not planned, wanted or welcome. I was never taught how to love and therefore I'm a woman of small words, or few words. This is why I want to write these words and though they are way overdue, I want to write them while I'm still alive.

I'm so sorry for not telling you how much you mean to me, how much I love you and how proud I am of you!

I also want to tell you that I am so sorry for all the hurt you've suffered and all you've been through.

I'm so sorry for all of the abuse; physical, mental, spiritual and yes, even sexual. I know what your father did to you. I do believe you. Maybe if I had had the courage to do something when you told me you would've been okay. If I had believed you sooner and left him, or ran away, or sought shelter for us you wouldn't have had to pay the price you paid. I was so young and feared for my life and yours. I was paralyzed with fear so I stayed.

I need to say I'm sorry. I believe you and I pray that you can forgive me so that I can rest in peace.
Love,
Mom

****

Dear Mommy,

I am so sorry for all past times that I have hurt you. Looking back on it now it hurts me to know that I have stolen from you a multiple of times. I am sorry for sneaking out in the summer and taking your truck and driving to see one of my friends in the middle of the night.

I am extremely sorry for always stealing money from your purse and buying minutes for my cell phone and for buying other things when I knew you needed the money more than I did.

I am really sorry that I would steal your cigarettes and I am really sorry I even started smoking. Mom, you are the best mother in the world and I would not want any other mother but you. I love you so much. I am so sorry for the things that were said, and for the countless times I told you to leave me alone. I really wanted you to talk to me.

Mommy I love you and I want to tell you exactly how I feel. I love everything that you have done for me. You have carried me for 9 months, and went through hours of labor for me. The day I was born was one of the happiest days of your life, you have told me that a million times.

Mommy I cannot emphasize enough how sorry I am for all the things I said to you when I was upset. I did not mean anything that I said, that's all that matters. I know deep in my heart you love me and that we can always depend on each other. I made it through the hard times thanks to your warm embrace and caring face.

Mom you were always there for me and I should have told you time and time again how much I love you. Whenever I was put down you were always there for me and I sometimes get misty eyed thinking about it.

Mom, I remember a letter that you sent me which said "Now I know that your father and I have made some mistakes raising you and I know I am not the best mother", that very line hit me like a ton of bricks and I remember I started crying.

Then I remember that I broke down and told you that you're the best mother in the world and I hate the fact that you feel or felt that way. Mom you are phenomenal and I would not want any other mother but you. Mommy, I love you and cherish you. I am so sorry for everything I have ever done to you.
Love,
Your Son

****

Letters of Apology

Dear Dad,

I write today to apologize to you. We don't talk much anymore. I always go straight to my room. I don't say hi to you when I come home. I often don't even acknowledge you exist. I have said I love you only twice in the past 9 years. I don't know where our relationship went, but now that I am getting older I regret loosing it more.

I lost all respect for you when I found out you smoked pot. I was only a child. You were my role model. I loved you. You were the greatest Dad. I thought you were a great person. To someone so young a great person is not a person that smokes pot. All of a sudden you were not the person I thought you were. You were not the Dad I wanted to have and all my love was lost.

Being so young, those are the things I thought. I tried to act like I hadn't found out; just go on with my life without showing you anymore love. Of course, if I didn't show you anymore love, I couldn't show anyone else either. I stopped communicating and slowly detached myself as a member of the family. I realize now, it's one of my biggest problems; communication. Maybe if I had just told you we could have worked it out and all would have been different. But I know I can't think like that. It doesn't help anything now. I can't fix what I did then even though I realize now it was wrong.

I know I should apologize to you, but I feel as if it's too late. The thing is, once it really is too late, I know I will regret not telling you now. And I'll know I could have done it, should have done it, would have done it and it will forever hurt me that I didn't. But I still cannot bring myself to do it.

The thing is I don't know exactly what I was thinking all those years ago. It wasn't just the fact that you smoked pot. I felt betrayed in so many ways. I had been raised to follow rules, but you weren't following the rules. I could not understand why you would damage your body and the rest of the family.

Letters of Apology

You hid it from me. You knew it was wrong, so you lied to me. Maybe you couldn't tell your daughter 'oh by the way I do drugs' but I couldn't understand and after that I lost a lot of trust in you.

I know justifying my actions doesn't change the fact that what I did was wrong. Never saying I love you has hurt you so much. I know it has, and you do so well to shower me with the small amount of love that I allow, even though I never show any in return.

There have been times when I changed my mind and decided to tell you I love you, but when the time came, I just couldn't.

As a daughter, I was never there for you when you needed me. I was never there to talk to. I was never there to hug. I was never there to say I love you. I fought with you all the time and treated you horribly. I apologize.

Dad, I want to say the hardest words possible to you because I know one day, I no longer will be able to no matter how much I want to.

I love you. I know I hurt you Daddy. I hope
I find the courage to make it all better before
it's too late.

Love,

Daddy's Girl

5.

Wishing, Waiting & Wanting

The easiest way to recognize when an apology is appropriate is to look at a situation like it's an equation. On one side of the equation we have people doing something. On the other side of the equation we have people dealing with the results. If the results of our actions have had a negative effect on a person, place or thing, chances are very good that someone owes somebody an apology.

We've all been on both sides of the apology equation and learned a few things in the process. Like how much easier it is to recognize when we're the one owed the apology than it is to admit it if we're the one who owes the apology.

We've also experienced the shift in power that sometimes takes place when the equation is created. It feels like the power to remedy the situation rests squarely in the hands of the person owing the apology.

We always have the choice of confronting that person, but more often than not, we give into our own self-doubt and find ourselves wishing, waiting or wanting for them to make the first move and apologize.

Wishing: We all know what wishing is; it's something we do when we don't have the faith or know-how to turn our dreams and desires into realities.

We wish for things like winning the lottery, becoming famous, a better job with better pay, better health or a bigger house. And sometimes we find ourselves wishing people would apologize for the things they've done or maybe the things they still do to us.

Either way, the damage we've experienced on the receiving end of the apology equation has been so severe, profound or prolonged that we've lost the ability to see the real reasons behind their actions and instead, accept the implication that we are the ones responsible for what happened to us.

They act as if they know the 'unpleasant truth' about us and even if we are able to muster up the courage to question them and the things they do, they are ready. They will twist their version of the truth to suit the situation, refuse to talk at all or threaten to expose our flaws and failings to the rest of the world.

We wish things would change, but we're at a loss of how to get them to change or stop what they're doing. We don't know how not to believe their interpretation of what happened or what continues to happen and as long as we believe even the tiniest particle of what they've implied about us, no other person will be able to convince us we deserve better; not even ourselves.

Waiting for an apology is a little bit better because even though our self image has been challenged, it hasn't been challenged enough for us to blindly accept the idea that we got what we deserved or that we don't deserve better.

The reason waiting isn't much better than wishing is because we still think the power to resolve the situation is in the hands of the person owing the apology.

The people on the other side of the equation are very often a part of our lives and for better or worse, its part of our human nature to trust the people we have a lot of history with to tell us the truth about what happened. Our roots are mingled with theirs and so are the roots of our desire to think of ourselves as worthy human beings.

When the people who know us the best don't apologize to us so we can relax and once again believe we're worthy of belonging and being loved, we will have to work extra hard to believe it on our own.

Waiting feels better than wishing because we think we're being proactive. We're waiting for something specific - an apology. But what we're really waiting for is for the people involved to have the ultimate *aha* moment when they are finally ready to admit they were wrong and that now they can see us as the worthy, good, descent, capable, lovable person we don't seem to be able to believe we are on our own.

Are we good, descent, kind, generous, lovable, worthy people? Of course we are; we are all worthy of belonging and being loved. There's just something so compelling about the way some of the people in our lives can consistently say and do things that make us feel like we're not worthy of being treated any better than they treat us now.

We aren't able to move forward because we're waiting to reconcile the things that have happened with them and if we can't reconcile those things, how can we ever hope to know how to reconcile what happens in the future with them or anybody else? We don't realize we've given them the power to decide what we do or don't deserve. Instead we wait for their apology as confirmation that they have finally seen the 'good truth' within us.

Wanting: When we want an apology our initial reaction still might be to wonder if we did something to deserve the negative result we experienced, but we don't automatically hand the power to make that decision over to the person who created the situation. Instead, we think about what happened and how we feel about it.

We may still decide we want an acknowledgement or an apology, but it won't be because we need it to confirm who's responsible for the situation. We already instinctively know who's responsible.

We want them to apologize because their actions have somehow excluded us. They've singled us out or pushed us out and we want back in. Their apology is the reassurance we seek to restore the belief that we belong and are loved by the people in our world. And sometimes, satisfying this need is more important to us than the things other people do to us.

Maybe wanting an apology isn't as bad as wishing or waiting for one, but even at its best, it's still just the lesser of three evils and we're still on the wrong side of the apology equation.

To varying degrees, each of the three situations is about the same thing, trying to recover a sense of security and self-worth that's been dinged, dented or demolished by something someone else did or said.

Needing an apology means we've fallen under the influence of what some people would prefer us to believe: that they have the right to determine our worth and value as a human being. But we are all worthy of being loved and of being treated with respect and dignity. No one has the right to take that away from us even if it sometimes feels like they have the power to do so.

****

Dear Wife,

You don't know how hard it is to write this letter. I have asked for forgiveness so many times. I have cried many tears when I think about what I did to you. You are the love of my life! You are an answer to a prayer, a perfect gift from God. Why I cheated on you, I can't explain. I can tell you that it had nothing to do with you and all to do with me.

I am so sorry for all the hurt, for all the pain, for how I let you down, for ruining your idea of a perfect husband. I love you and regret all the tears and the time of interrupted love because of what I did.

Love,
Your one and only Love

****

41

Dear Daughter,

I'm so sorry for the things I said and did to you. Sometimes, there were times back then when I was so unhappy and so angry and I know I was just awful to you. There you were, this beautiful, smart energized little girl who looked just like I did when I was your age and it made me so mad and I don't even know why, but there were times when I just couldn't even look at you or talk to you or anything without feeling all this anger and frustration and then I would say and do things to you that were so unkind and hurtful and I am so very sorry for all of it.

You have such a wonderful spirit and you've grown into a wonderful human being full of love. Everything you do will be based with this and every life you touch will be blessed for knowing you.

Please don't let the things I've done or said have any effect on you. You can do whatever you want and whatever you contribute will make the world a better place.

I love you in my heart. I am proud of you and all you have accomplished and all you will accomplish.

I love you,

Mom

****

Dear Friend,

I know you are angry with me because of my last letter and I'm sorry for that, but you need to look at this from my side. When I wrote you the last letter regarding your drinking problem, it was only after I had witnessed how much worse your drinking problem had become. It looked like you were unable to stop drinking. You even got up at 4:00am because you needed a drink and it really scared me. I have asked you many times to seek help and stop drinking. You always agree, change the subject and then keep drinking.

When I came home after my last visit with you, all I could think about was how you were ruining your life and killing yourself. You tried to

Letters of Apology

show me a good time, but watching the state you were in was painful. You were so drunk you confused night with day and started to get ready for work at 7:00 pm.

You were my good friend but your drinking has completely taken over. I felt like I had to help you stop destroying your life. I wrote that last letter as an intervention, not to hurt you but to try and reach you. I wrote the letter because I care, if I didn't care I wouldn't have done anything. I realize the letter was poorly worded and I should have been more positive about what you have going for you like your beautiful home, a job you love, your sense of humor, your kindness and generosity. I guess I was just trying to hit you hard hoping it would shake you up enough to get you to see how much better your life would be if you stopped drinking.

I don't know what else I can say. I'm sorry about the letter, I think about you often and sincerely hope that you are doing well.

Your friend

6.

It's not your fault

Without a doubt, none of us enjoys finding ourselves on the wrong side of the apology equation regardless of how we got there.

It doesn't matter if we got there as the result of a miscommunication, someone else's minor mistake or the result of someone else's ridiculously unacceptable behavior. All of these situations can be unpleasant and uncomfortable and when we find ourselves caught up in them our instinct is very often to wonder what we did wrong.

We've been drawn into someone else's drama and once we start thinking from this perspective it's hard to shift our attention to any other. We want to understand what happened and we think that if we can figure out what we did wrong, then we might be able to fix things and prevent this type of thing from ever happening again.

Unfortunately when we spend our time trying to understand what we did wrong, we lose sight of the simple truth: ***people do what they do for their own reasons.***

If someone did something and we suffered as a result, regardless of whether that was their intention or not, their decision to act was influenced by their private agendas, both conscious and unconscious and made in the quiet solitude of their mind.

We might have provided input, but it doesn't make any difference what our input was; any action they took was based on a decision they made for their own private reasons.

After the damage is done, we might think 'hey, that hurt, you owe me an apology.' And maybe someone should apologize for the hurt or harm we experienced as a result of their action, but if we decide their action was because of us or because of something we did or said, then that's a decision we make based on the conscious and unconscious agendas residing in the quiet solitude of our own mind.

What if, instead of taking someone else's actions personally and letting the chain reaction continue throughout our day – or worse – our life, we were able to stop long enough to remind ourselves that people do what they do because of the things going on in their life?

Obviously, there are some behaviors that are unacceptable regardless of the rationalizations taking place between one person's ears. But as soon as we decide to consider what might be going on for someone else, we'll realize there are times when the negative impact we feel is the result of our perspective rather than the result of someone else's genuine intent to cause us hurt or harm.

Granted, it takes a little time and practice to stop reacting to people and their actions, especially if we have history with them. But if we can delay our reaction long enough to wonder what might be going on for someone else, we'll see unexpected things like sadness, frustration, anxiety, exhaustion, anger, fear, etc.; all of which probably have nothing to do with us.

And when we take the time to consider what might be going on for someone else, we are less likely to jump to the conclusion that we are responsible for their actions.

Of course this means that we're also going to be more aware of times when our own actions are about to unleash a little unpleasantness in someone else's direction because of what's going on for us. But then we'll realize it's just one more thing we have in common with each other.

None of us is perfect, we are all just trying to make our way in the world, and we all make mistakes along the way.

****

Dear Teacher,

I would like to apologize for all the times I went to school and didn't do my work. I didn't do my work because I was acting like a fool and talking to my friends. Sometimes when I come to class I feel lazy and I don't have my head in place. Other times students will distract me.

I think I should do my work and pay attention to you. I will try not to talk to people and try to complete my work. Also I will not sit next to students that distract me, and if I do not understand my work I will ask you for help.

I would like to apologize for my behavior and I would like to thank you for being a good teacher. I like it when you help me when I do not understand my work, and I appreciate you encouraging me and telling me when I do well. I understand that you need to discipline me when I'm doing something wrong.

I hope you forgive me for my behavior and I will continue to try my best. You are a great person and a good teacher. Please continue to care about your students because your caring has made a difference in my life.
Sincerely,
Your Student.

****

To my ex-husbands mistress,

Now that time has passed and I have moved on, I wish I could apologize for a couple of things. I'm not sorry I was mad at you. I had every right to be mad at you. What I want to apologize for is for blaming you. Blaming you accomplished nothing and if my marriage had been stronger, you wouldn't have been there in the first place.

The second thing I want to say I'm sorry for is for verbally trashing you to your face and behind your back. When I think about it now it's plain to me we were both victims. We were both used and lied to over and over again. Maybe I had a right to yell at you, but I didn't need to be so mean and deliberately hurtful while doing it.

I hope you learned as much about yourself from what happened as I did. Anyway, I'm sorry.
Sincerely,
You know who

7.

No Really, It's not Your Fault

Once we accept the idea that people act according to their own private, personal agendas our world starts to change for the better. We get better at recognizing the difference between reacting and responding to other people's actions.

Now when someone unleashes unpleasantness in our direction we know to pause and consider what might be going on for them before responding. With practice we might even begin to feel sympathy or a genuine empathy for what other people are struggling with even when their actions clearly lack any reverse consideration for how we might feel about what they're doing.

Life would definitely be easier if our new perspective would automatically create a similar shift in perspective for the person we are at odds with. But it's unlikely they will stop repeating behaviors that have always produced the result they desire. And some behaviors, especially ones with history are still going to make us flinch in spite of our best effort to respond rather than react.

What's much more likely is for them to continue and sometimes even escalate their behavior when our response is suddenly different from what they're used to.

As they persist and try harder, our role in the dance becomes perfectly clear; they expect us to follow and allow them to lead without question. And once this light of awareness goes on for us, it stays on.

Now we have a conundrum: how can we continue to be part of a situation when the other person persists in their belief that their actions are completely justified now that we've realized it's all about them and has nothing to do with us?

We're likely to start by rationalizing that we're strong enough to survive what they're dishing out. We know they're struggling with their issues and we're getting better at not taking their issues personally, so that should be enough to help us get through the tough times, right? After all we've survived up until now and that's without the benefit of all this new insight.

Maybe we'll make a conscious decision to stay because we believe we can help, fix, change or otherwise alter the situation enough for the light of awareness to go on for the other person.

We might start reading self help books. Some of us will even rationalize putting our own lives and hopes of personal happiness on hold while we search for the one perfect answer that will make all the difference for someone else.

Unfortunately even the most perfect, rational answer will be meaningless to a person who can't or won't listen to what we're saying.

Bottom line - we can stick around and suffer through all of it, but even when our intentions are as honest and pure as crocuses in springtime, no amount of suffering on our part will ever help, cure, save or fix someone else.

On the one hand, this is a complicated realization. It means there are some relationships we should consider letting go of because staying in them means we are accepting the risk of letting a part of us die.

On the other hand, we have learned something very important. We have a choice now. And whether we choose to continue with all, part, or none of the relationship, just knowing that people do what they do for their own private reasons, will help diminish the impact of their past, present and future actions.

Granted, it would still be nice to get an apology, but at least now we can start to unravel the mystery of negative situations and limit their uncanny ability to send us into a downward spiral thinking less and less of ourselves with each occurrence.

Now we have a new perspective to view our world with; and with practice, the ability to avoid getting caught up and ultimately trapped in the destructive dramas of other people.

****

Dear Soulful Artist:

I just walked away from seven years with you. I never returned your phone calls and answered your e-mails with so few words. I knew that by ignoring your hurt I would hurt you deeply. I am writing to admit my part in this tragic love story. I was not ready for such a deep level of commitment as a couple. I so enjoyed our time together, but I had so many fears about moving forward. You were right about that.

Sometimes, we don't "recognize the sweet cream when all we've had is skim milk".

I'm sorry I ignored your pain and I wish you Love & Light Always.....

Your Muse

****

Dear Friend,

This is a difficult but necessary letter for me to write. Many years ago, when we were still close and trusted friends, I betrayed your love, friendship, trust and loyalty by having a brief sexual relationship with your boyfriend.

I'm not sure why I did it; I wasn't even very attracted to him. I think partly because I'd always been envious of your beauty, strength, confidence and competence, and partly because I was flattered that your boyfriend was showing an interest in me.

There's no excuse and it's been one of the most shameful and regrettable things I've ever done, something I haven't been able to forgive myself for.

I am so very, very sorry,
A former friend

8.

Weeds

Weeds will try to take root in any garden; even the best gardens and they can be so temptingly disarming when they first appear. So much so that sometimes we let one sneak in and watch it grow and blossom without realizing it's slowly and silently choking the life out of the garden surrounding it.

Life too, offers a surprisingly wide variety of 'weeds' for us to contend with. Our job is to learn how to identify the weeds native to us and our world so we can deal with them before they get out of control and we realize they're choking the life out of us.

Repeat Offenders: These are the people who continue to do the things they do regardless of how the results of their behaviors affect the people around them. It can start simply enough; they do something that has a negative effect on us but instead of bringing it to their attention or making sure they're aware of how we really feel about what they did, we cut them some slack and let it slide.

The situation goes away and then all of a sudden they do it again. If we bring it to their attention they may disagree and tell us their actions were completely justified or that they can't control themselves long enough to not do whatever they are doing. They may even promise to try and not do it again.

We could continue to make a fuss, but most of us decide to be the 'bigger person', cut them some more slack and once again let it slide. Still not too big of a problem until it happens again, again, and again.

By now the repeat offender has entered their comfort zone because even though we may complain about what they do, we're still here. Our logical brain will remind us that we can always walk away from the situation, but we're invested by now.

So instead of taking a walk we let our instincts tempt us with thoughts of helping them, fixing them, or giving them the time and space they need to work through their problems.

The People We Feel Obligated to Love: These are the people in our lives who, by virtue of our relationship with them, we are inclined to love and/or respect. They populate our world and we use the results of our interactions with them to help us define ourselves.

We get used to being in each other's lives and when these relationships are good we fall into patterns of behavior that can be comfortable and reassuring. When these people hear us talk about our ideas, plans or dreams they respond with enthusiasm and encourage us even if it means change for them too.

But when these relationships are troubled, the patterns we fall into can be challenging and painful. If we try to change them, change what they're doing to us or try to put some distance between us, the people involved aren't likely to cooperate.

Instead, they're likely to say and do things to discourage us. They are quick to dismiss our ideas and concerns, downplay our abilities or just plain guilt us into staying right where we are. They will do what they have to do to maintain the predictability of their life regardless of what it might mean to us and our life.

The Perpetual Button Pusher: We all have perpetual button pushers in our lives and of all the things we face button pushing is one of the most challenging because it's not just about us; it's about us and at least one other person. Button pushers are the people who seem to know exactly what to do to annoy us – and they do it; sometimes relentlessly.

It helps to know they're doing it for their own reasons, but our knowing won't stop them from doing and it's going to take a while for us to realize our actions are actually reactions to someone pushing our buttons.

Like actors on Broadway, we've learned our parts by heart and can act them out on autopilot. After that, even an innocent comment by a stranger can get us to respond with line and verse.

We can decide to change or alter our behavior, stop consciously believing in the justifications they throw our way, do the things a better would person do or whatever; that doesn't mean they're going to cooperate.

In fact, they might even push harder because when we don't react the way they want us to, something in their world isn't right and they're going to do what they need to do to get back into their comfort zone.

We get frustrated because regardless of what we try, we continue to get caught up in their chain reaction of events and it begins to feel like it's never going to change; not the people, not the situation, not our ability to get away from it.

People Who've Had a Tough Life: We all face challenges in our lives, but some people have had more bad or unfortunate luck fall their way. As a result, they may have adopted curious and sometimes dysfunctional ways of dealing with their history.

When we know their story, or their struggle is obvious, our instincts are to be compassionate even if we are the recipient of their negative results.

Unfortunately some of these people prefer to live their lives in a perpetually dysfunctional state of denial. They do things because of their past but don't, won't or can't acknowledge the source of their behavior.

We are challenged because there's a fine line between cutting someone slack for having had a tough life and letting someone continue to cause us hurt or harm when they don't, won't or can't acknowledge the damage they're doing.

Really Bad People: It's one of the unfortunate realities we live with; there are people who do bad things, sometimes really bad things. We could stop and debate nature versus nurture but it won't matter which side wins. If a really bad person manages to maneuver, manipulate or force their way into our life it's going to be a bumpy ride.

We might be tempted to try and make sense of what happened, but trying to understand someone else's reasons for putting our safety and sanity at risk is a waste of time. There are some things people shouldn't do regardless of their reasons and no matter how hard someone might try to impose their justifications on us, it's never okay to *intentionally* cause hurt or harm.

All of these people have played or continue to play a role in our lives and before we know it we'll start looking at the people around us to see if they fit into one of these groups. We might even start a mental inventory of who we think we would like an apology from.

So we start our inventory, but pretty quickly a light comes on and we find ourselves wondering what group the people we know would put us into. Are we button pushers? Are we someone else's repeat offender?

****

Dearest Love,

I love you so and I am so grateful for your love.

I am sorry for everything that I ever said or did to cause you pain. I'm just so afraid of love and getting hurt. Deep down I love you so much and I have nothing but love and respect for you, but sometimes it's hard to tell because I try so hard to hide my true feelings out of fear. When I'm fearful, it causes me to say and do hurtful things, like walking away from you and leaving you. I should never have let you down like that.

These past weeks have allowed me to really look inside myself and be honest about who I am and how I feel. I'm trusting God to take care of us, to heal our hurts and fears. Now I have learned that we are love and that it's okay for me to let my heart love and to be loved. And I am learning to love myself profoundly as I love you. Do what makes you happy my love.

I love you so.

Your Love

****

To the people I've hurt in the past,
I'm sorry for what I did to all of you.
I'm sorry for all the times I cheated on my
girlfriends.
I'm sorry for what I did to my best friends too.
I lied to everyone and I'm sorry for all of it,
forever.
I hope all of you can forgive me.

****

To my Children,

    I know growing up without a father
must have been hard and it had to be doubly
hard knowing that your father was an addict
too. I know now that there must have been
times when you needed to know you were safe
and that dad was there to protect you, but I
wasn't. I was off doing my own thing
thinking only of myself. Not only was that
selfish, but it was wrong too. I don't know if
you will ever forgive me, but I want you to
know that I am truly and deeply sorry for the
hurt I caused you.

Your Dad

Letters of Apology

9.

When Good People
do Bad Things

It's not easy to turn the tables and put ourselves under the same microscope we've started to put everyone else under. But their truth is our truth: everything we do, everything we've done, we've done for our own reasons and we would be foolish to even consider the idea that we have not hurt and/or harmed people in our life along the way.

When we realize this our attention will start shifting from thinking about our encounters with other people to thinking about encounters other people have had with us.

Some memories will make us smile because we all do good things. But others will make us cringe and we'll remember why we choose to push them into the dark corners of our mind. As long as they stay there, we can continue to pretend we've never put a look of disbelief on someone else's face, caused the pain reflected in someone else's eyes, seen the angry expression of betrayal or heard hurt echoing through a shaky voice.

These are challenging memories regardless of which side of the apology equation we've experienced them from, but they're especially challenging when we're the one responsible for them.

Just the thought of dredging up things we've done in the past is enough to stop a lot of us. After all, we've managed to survive up until now with all those unpleasant memories neatly tucked away, surely a few more decades of denial won't matter.

Maybe, but making the decision to look at our past doesn't mean we have to dissect it. We can if we want to, but digging through unpleasant memories, reviewing old justifications and rationalizations or searching for new insights will not change the past.

Damage done is damage done and if we were the ones responsible for the damage then we did what we did for our own private reasons as a result of our own conscious and unconscious agendas. We may be able to personalize the 'why', but that's it; after that we're just like every other human being on the planet, and they're just like us.

This is everybody's truth. We are all a collage of people and situations; a diverse mixture of the good, the bad and the ugly.

Knowing this, how will we view the things we've done now? How will we feel when we realize that there have been times when we've pursued our agendas at someone else's expense?

Probably not very good. It's much more likely that when we start to think about the negative things we've done and how those things might have made other people feel we'll experience one of those other emotions like regret, remorse, shame, embarrassment, guilt, etc....

And when we genuinely feel bad about the things we've done or said, even though we probably felt completely justified at the time, it will be easier for us to accept the thought that maybe the people who hurt or harmed us are capable of realizing how their actions made us feel.

Granted, they may not be ready or able to acknowledge those feelings or put them into words, but we probably weren't at one point in time either.

****

Dear Mom,

During your dying days, I am so sorry that I wasn't there for you as often as you wanted me to be. I was falling apart at the thought of your death and just couldn't handle it the way both of us would've preferred.

At 67, the age I'm at now, you were much too young to die, especially since you enjoyed living as much as you did. And the thought of losing my mother whom I dearly loved and whose company I enjoyed, was "killing me."

Nearly thirty years later, I still miss you and am envious of my friends whose parents are still living. I love you and miss you.

Love,
Your daughter

****

To my poor body,
I know that there is no excuse for the abuse I have dished out over the years.

Although I know that you are the only body I will be given, I have constantly tortured and sometimes ignored you completely.

I have given you too much sun, food, smoke, drink and sometimes absolutely nothing to live on.

I have ignored your screams of pain and your desire for rest and healing.

I am so sorry for my desire to eat empty calories, fatty foods and junk.

I hated looking at you for years. In my efforts to change you I starved you, I threw up, I hated you.

You were always just a reflection of my diseased mind. I cannot make up for my mistakes with words.

My commitment to you is that I will think of health first at all times.

I won't be perfect-- 50 years of old habits die hard and sometimes the mental obsession is very strong.

I promise to get support and not hide you when I can't help myself.

I promise you more days of healthful eating, rest, sunscreen and regular but not crazy exercise.

I promise to try to spread the idea of healthy living to my children and my children's children.

I promise to take care of you from here until the day I can no longer take care of myself.

Me

****

Dear God,

I'm sorry. I'm struggling because there are so many things wrong with my life and I want to pray to you for help, but I don't feel like I have the right because of all the things I've screwed up in my life. How can I ask you for help now when I haven't done a very good job with the help you've given me in the past?

I can't imagine what I look like to you right now. But please look inside me because if you do you'll see how truly sorry I am for not doing better.

I really am trying.

10.

A New Beginning

We all make mistakes. We all do things we should apologize for and one of the reasons these letters are so powerful is because we can all recognize bits and pieces of ourselves and our lives within them.

Between the lines of all these various situations are the words so many of us have hoped for: that we deserved better, that it wasn't our fault, that the person or people responsible are truly and sincerely sorry.

There are some good feelings we connect with these words too; relief, joy, excitement, even emancipation. But what happens next? Even if we're one of the lucky ones and get a sincere, person-to-person apology will it change our lives?

With apology in hand will we finally be able to put the past behind us and suddenly be filled with the self-believe that we really are the person we've always dreamed of being?

We can wait a minute, a month or a lifetime for the apology we think we need, but there isn't an apology on the planet with the power to make any one of us someone other than whom we choose to be. And even if we do get it, the face we see in the mirror the morning after the apology is going to be the same face we saw in the mirror the morning before the apology.

We don't want to think about what doesn't change with an apology though. We'd rather think about what will change and how much nicer things will be between us.

An apology will be offered, we will accept it, the apology equation will be dissolved and our relationships will be restored and renewed.

It's certainly easier to quantify the situation this way than it is to worry about what the situation says about us as a person or what it says about our relationships with the person or people on the other side of the equation.

But our lives revolve around our relationships with each other; we share our goals, dreams and agendas and grow to trust each other.

When the apology equation is set up it means we've fallen out of sync with each other and it's the value we place on the relationship that will determine how long we're willing to wait or what we're willing to overlook while we wait for the situation to be resolved.

If we didn't care about our relationship with the person or people involved, we wouldn't care whether we did or didn't get an apology.

Waiting is stressful because we're not just waiting for an apology; we're waiting for someone else to tell us via an apology whether or not they value their relationship with us as much as we value our relationship with them. If they give us an apology, they do.

If they don't give us an apology we won't know if they care about us, our feelings or how much of our relationship will be affected by this situation. Will the disruption carry over into other areas of our relationship or will we get over this trouble spot and pick up right where we left off?

The mistake we make is in thinking that not getting an apology means they don't like, love or care about us or our relationship with them. We need to remind ourselves that most people don't intentionally try to hurt or harm others.

If someone isn't willing to resolve an apology equation they are responsible for, it's evidence of a personal agenda. They are trapped by it; they can't say they're wrong, they can't say we're right, they can't even agree to disagree. All they can do is continue to stand their ground until they are able to recognize, come to terms with or let go of whatever it is they are holding onto.

We on the other hand don't have to wait for an apology. All we have to do is remember two things: we are the same person with or without an apology and they are doing what they are doing because of who they are, not because of who we are.

This doesn't mean we aren't accountable for what we might have added to a situation; it just means we aren't required to let ourselves be held hostage by other people's agendas.

In the beginning it takes a little practice to become aware of when we are caught or about to be caught up in an apology equation, but there is a quick way to become proficient at recognizing these situations. Pay attention to when we are on the *other* side of the apology equation; the side where we owe the apology.

As we start recognizing situations when we need to apologize for the negative results we've created, we'll start getting better at recognizing situations when we're about to get sucked into someone else's equation.

The sooner we start getting better at not letting our personal agendas get in the way of us apologizing the sooner we'll begin to understand that the magical, healing power of an apology isn't felt just by the person receiving it, it's also felt by the person offering it.

Every time we wrap the seven magic words around a situation we've created and offer them to the person or people involved, we're not just saying we're sorry, we're saying that we value our relationship with them, that they deserve better, that it wasn't their fault, that they are worthy and that we are truly and sincerely sorry if we did something that made them feel otherwise.

When we tell the people in our lives this, then maybe, when they look in the mirror tomorrow morning it will be easier for them to see and believe these truths too.

****

Dear _____,

As I write this letter I realize I don't know when you'll be reading it. I wish I could give it to you right now, but I don't have that kind of courage right now.

I'm writing this letter to say I'm sorry for all the things I did to you. I wish I could explain why I did them, but I can't. Even if I could, they'd still be nothing more than excuses.

I don't know if saying I'm sorry now will make any difference. I only know that it's important to me you know that I've looked at the things I've done and realize there's no excuse that could ever make our past okay.

I decided to write this letter because I've been trying to be a better person (even though I don't feel like I deserve it most of the time).

Thinking about the things I've done makes me feel like crap and if I can still remember them then chances are you remember them and that makes me feel worse.

I was wrong for the things I did and said and I feel like crap because I dragged you into it. I could tell you I didn't know any better or that I treated you that way because that's the way the people in my life treated me, but that's just another stupid excuse and I want to stop using my past as an excuse.

I wish there were perfect words to make it better, but I don't know what the perfect words are. I can only say these words over and over and hope they are good enough.

I'm so very, very sorry for all the bad, hurtful things I ever said or did to you. You never did anything to deserve any of them.

Letters of Apology

It's not like you had any choice, because you didn't. It was all my doing. If I could take it all back I would, but I can't, I can't change any of it and I'm sorry for that too.

I hate that I can't fix this and I hate thinking about how much you must hate me even though I know you have every right to hate me.

Just to be clear about one thing, I'm not asking you to forgive me. You may never be able to. That's not why I'm writing this letter. I'm writing this letter because I wanted to be sure you knew that you were innocent. You didn't bring any of what I did on yourself. You didn't earn any of it. You didn't deserve any of it. There is nothing wrong with you. It was all me and there is nothing you could have done to change me or stop me. That is the truth.

The other reason I wanted to write this letter is because I realized that none of us knows when our time is up. Every day I remember the things I've done not just to you, but to other people too.

I'm done trying to hide from the things I've done and the thought of you never knowing how deeply I regret what happened between you and me started to drive me crazy. You deserve to know. You deserve to hear the words. You deserve to have them in your hand.

I hope somewhere in this letter I've managed to convince you that I really mean what I'm saying. If I didn't get it exactly right then I'm sorry for that too. But please believe me when I say, from the bottom of my heart that I am truly and completely sorry for all of it. You are a good person, you were not responsible and if I could live all those years over again I would take every opportunity I was given to tell you that you deserve to be treated with love and respect.

Like I said, I don't know if we'll ever have this conversation face to face, but at least you'll have this letter and maybe if you can read it more than once you will begin to believe what I've said. You are a good person, a better person than I was or could ever be.

I probably don't have the right to say this, but I love you and am proud of you and truly hope your life is filled with good people, good health, success and lots and lots of love. You deserve the best of everything life has to offer.

Your _____ .

11.

Edge of the World Thinking

There is a concept in psychology called **Reframing**. There are plenty of formal definitions for this concept, but a basic explanation is that you hold a thought in your mind that you believe to be true until a new piece of information makes you reconsider what you once believed.

A great example of reframing is what happened to people who used to believe the earth was flat – and let's be serious – there was a time in the history of human beings when people truly believed the world was as flat as a pancake until it was proved otherwise.

People who grew up believing the world was flat experienced a reframing of their perspective when it was proved to them that the world was round.

In this situation the shift was so absolute that it disintegrated the previous perspective. Once they knew the world was round, they couldn't go back to living like it was flat.

That doesn't mean they didn't experience fear when they got on a ship to sail off into a big blue horizon. It does mean they didn't let their fears hold them back.

Reading a book like *Letters of Apology* puts us in a similar situation. We'd like to believe there is truth in the ideas presented, but before we can integrate them into our minds and lives our fight or flight instincts have to be convinced they are not life threatening.

As part of nature's defense system, fight or flight instincts are an innate safeguard designed to help us survive potentially harmful and/or lethal situations.

These instincts serve a very primal purpose. They exist because we are vulnerable human beings. Who can guess where human beings would be without their innate fight or flight instincts.

If an elephant charges in our direction the danger is obvious and our feelings of fear are definitely justified. The charging elephant provides us with a type of objective physical evidence our instincts can comprehend. Our instincts kick in and we get out of the way.

Our fight or flight instincts are always running in the background scanning for danger to the safety and security of our physical selves. Unfortunately our experience with instinct has led to confusion with our understanding of fear.

In the same way that our fight or flight instincts scan to protect our external being, our minds scan for threats to our internal safety and security. If we don't understand what going on, or can't make sense of what's happening or what happened with our mind, then our mind begins to think there might be something to be afraid of.

A fear could be nothing more than a minds response to the unknown in the absence of an instinctual fight or flight response. Being able to distinguish the difference between our fight or flight instincts and our fears is not an easy task because they can feel very much alike.

When a new idea is presented to our mind it tries to find a place to fit in. It's initially scanned for potential threats to the safety and security of our external world by our fight or flight instincts. If it survives the scrutiny of our instincts, it still has to get past the fear of the unknown test our mind applies.

Neither one of these two filters is great at analysis though. Their main duty is to scan for threats; they don't scan for the positive potential an idea might possess. Their focus is on maintaining the safety and security of a world we are currently surviving.

For them it's all black and white: as long as we continue to do what we've been doing and think what we've been thinking the world we're currently surviving will remain intact. Change creates a different unknown outcome and the unknown is a threat.

As strange as it might sound change is the enemy of our fears. To maintain our world as it is, in their own warped and twisted ways our instincts and fears will try to influence us to think and act in the same ways we always have to keep us from falling off the edge of a world they still perceive as flat.

Ultimately their one true benefit is also their one true downfall because…

Fears are about how to *survive*; they are not about how to *thrive*.

As long as we stare at the same blue horizon from the same dock talking about the same things as everyone else around us everything is fine.

It's a busy world though and if you don't pay attention you could wake up one day and find yourself surrounded by *'Caution: Edge of the World'* signs your fears have posted and disguised as comfort zones.

We don't realize we've been waiting for permission to extend our lives beyond these signs until a new idea or a new way of thinking enters our mind and we begin to consider what else might be out there.

On the other hand we do know what can happen if we start talking to the people in our lives about a new thought or way of thinking.

We're feeling hopeful and excited as we share the idea that there might be a dock, a beach or a whole new world on the other side of the mysterious blue horizon and that we've been thinking about heading out there to check it out for ourselves.

We have hopes for their response, but instead, in their own way, with their own words and reactions their response isn't what we had hoped for. We don't realize our words have presented a challenge to the shared reality necessary to maintain the safety and security of our shared world.

It's not that we've shared our ideas with the wrong people or that they are bad people; they just have their own edge of the world fears to deal with too. They may listen purposefully, but our words can be a trigger to the safety and security of the world they are currently surviving. The simple fact is most people just aren't ready to make the trip.

Knowing this might discourage us from talking out loud about our hopes and dreams but it doesn't always stop us from sitting and letting our feet dangle off the edge of the dock while we stare off into our own personal blue horizon and wonder if there really is something better out there.

We'll try to hold onto our dreams and internalize them before they slip away but our fears push us and the world around us pushes us until the combined consistent, persistent and hypnotic pulse of the world we know we can survive has its way with us.

We haven't necessarily given up because we're afraid. Our fears don't always make us afraid; sometimes they just make the status quo of our current lives feel safer than the unknown.

Why plot a course into the big blue unknown when you can survive right where you are? Why endanger yourself that way? It may sound exiting, but what happens if you're wrong and you really are sailing to the edge of the world? Falling off the edge of the world is not safe; staying right where we are is.

The tendency to maintain the world exactly as it is can be so subtle that we don't even realize we've slipped back into that two dimensional place where we don't trust ourselves, we believe it when people tell us we are wrong, everyone else is right and this dock really is the only dock we will ever need.

But now you've been reading about an idea known as reframing and this is the kind of idea that can change your life – *if you let it*.

Now that you've heard about reframing you can choose to realize that whenever a new idea enters your mind you are likely to encounter resistance in the form of fear.

It doesn't really matter when, where or how a fear originated; you might not ever know how it came into being. What does matter is understanding how our fears work to manipulate and influence our behavior.

Fear creates its own form of tension and it requires this tension to exist. It's like a tug-of-war except that fear has us convinced it's on our side helping us maintain enough tension on the rope to keep us from being pulled off or from falling off the edge of the world.

It comes disguised with the same undercurrent of imminent danger feelings we associate with our flight or flight instincts. It tries to convince us that it's here to protect us from a future pain or danger our senses can't perceive.

What would happen if we just dropped the tug-of-war rope? What could be different in your life if you realized you could look at a situation and actually decide between actions you consciously chose on your own or the reactions generated by your fears?

What could be different if you became aware that when you feel like you can't do anything right or like you have no control to fix things or like you'll never really be able to let go of the past it might be because your fears are trying to keep you right where you are.

If fear had a motto, it would go something like this: don't tempt fate; don't rock the boat; suck it up; stop being so selfish; you're not that lucky; just because you can't see it doesn't mean it isn't there.

Scary movie shows us over and over again what happens to characters who ignore the voice of fear in their heads and climb down those stairs into the dark and creepy cellar. They may encounter different outcomes when they get down there, but they're all bad.

It's tough to do something different with all those defensive rationalizations within our own minds working so hard to convince us that the fear we feel is justified.

What we need to remember is that if our fight or flight instincts aren't giving us the danger signal then chances are pretty good we may not be in a life or death situation.

There is a story about inhabitants of an island who one day saw something on the horizon they had never seen before. The islanders gathered on the shore trying to figure out what they were seeing and what they should do about it.

Over time the mysterious vision continued to grow larger but it wasn't until it was close to the island that the inhabitants were able to figure out that they were seeing some type of really big boat. All their island boats were small and open; these were boats of a size and complexity the islanders had never even imagined.

They weren't able to recognize them on the horizon because they had never seen large ships on the horizon before. From that point forward though, when that vision appeared on the horizon, they knew what they were looking at.

When we look into our big blue horizon we don't always know exactly what we're looking at. But that's okay. Just because we don't know or understand something doesn't automatically mean it's something we should be afraid of.

The idea that *people do what they do for their own reasons* is an idea that's out on the horizon for a lot of people and each of us will react to it in our own unique way. We might be excited about it while the person sitting right next to us is paralyzed with fear at the very thought of it even though we are looking at the exact same thing.

When this happens it helps to remember that our fears are specific to us. If they weren't we'd all be able to apply the same generic bandage and all our collective fears would be gone.

It also helps to remember that our minds can only hold one thought at a time. If we choose to focus on the possibilities then we will be thinking about possibilities. On the other hand if we let our fears take control we will find ourselves thinking a plethora of fearful thoughts.

95

One of the biggest reasons this idea is such a challenge is because it is a stepping stone to letting go of other people's perceptions about us. These perceptions are the ammunition our fears use as evidence of our inability to change or grow.

We all want to believe and feel like we are enough. We'd like to believe we can do something that will make a difference in the world or at least in the lives of the people around us.

We want to believe we can fix things that went wrong because that's the kind of person we truly are on the inside.

The flaw of this desire is that we look to other people for confirmation that we are enough and that we really can make a difference. The fear is that none of the people in our life will ever see us the way we wish they would and that they are right and we are wrong.

The truth is that as long as we give credence to any tiny particle of the fear that the people who hurt or harmed us did so because of who we are, because we deserved it or because we can never get it right, we will remain stuck on that dock blind to any other possibility.

Change and personal growth can be scary things when you consider pursuing them. But that's what life is, change and personal growth and this is your opportunity to prove this truth to yourself. Write a letter of apology.

Now before one of the nameless, faceless fears in your mind goes completely nuts and starts yelling at you to close this book, it's not a letter of apology to someone, it's the letter of apology *owed to you*.

Write the apology you've given up any hope of ever getting; the apology you've been owed for what seems like forever.

Write it without thinking about it too much. Just write, don't edit. Make it as long as it needs to be. Put in as much detail as you want. Include all their excuses and reasons and make sure it includes those 7 magic words so it really is the complete and total apology you've wanted to hear for so long.

No one else ever has to read it. This letter is for you and only you. Make sure it's written from the perspective of the person who owes you the apology. You don't need their input or their permission to write it.

You might find that another fear is chiming in and trying to convince you that you don't have to literally write the letter; that thinking about it is enough, but that's not true. We don't just learn by thinking, we learn just as much if not more by doing.

Just write one letter of apology you are owed. When you're done writing, read. Read it more than once. If you've really written the letter you wanted, reading it will be very compelling. After all, it is all the words you've been waiting for and here they are in your hands.

Now, what do you want to believe? Do you want to believe a nameless faceless fear trying to convince you that there is no way this is real or will you believe me when I tell you without any doubt or hesitation that this apology totally, absolutely and completely exists in the heart of the person who owes it you?

If they haven't offered you an apology it isn't because of who you are, it's because of who they are and because of the fears that continue to rule their life.

If you need more corroboration, take another look at the letters in this book. All those people sharing their heartfelt apologies with *you* just so *you* can believe that the apology in your hand is real.

Allow yourself at least one moment to believe this and see what happens. As soon as we start letting other people make mistakes instead of thinking we're the only ones who can't get things right, past situations just start to disintegrate. We realize we don't need their permission to be the person we were born to be. Those situations can only hold us hostage for as long as we let them.

We might also realize that the whole time we've been wishing, wanting and waiting for an apology we have been holding them hostage too. In the same way that we've been waiting for permission to think better things about ourselves, maybe they may have been wishing, wanting and waiting for us to give them permission to not be the person who did those things.

Fears require tension to exist. Reading *Letters of Apology*, believing in the sincerity of the letters within it and writing a letter of apology gives each one of us an opportunity to think and act beyond all the limits that have been quietly keeping us right where we are.

Accepting the idea that a sincere apology lives within the heart of all human beings is a choice we get to make. The world can be a harsh place to live and people do things, sometimes bad things, but nothing we do can change the heart of who we are. It's always there, our true selves, on the inside patiently waiting for us to find our way. We don't need anybody else's permission to go there.

It doesn't matter if our journey takes us in different directions, what matters is that we share the knowledge of a wonderful truth - we are all descent human beings worthy of belonging and being loved.

Dear Mommy,

   I am really really sorry
I made you cry.
   Please don't be mad at
me.
   I love you,

   Truly Yours,

   Me

Thank you so much for reading *Letters of Apology*. My hope is that you have been empowered, encouraged and inspired by the ideas and people represented here. Every person who contributed a letter openly shared a part of their private, personal history hoping that it might, in some way, help all of us.

If you would like to share any feelings, opinions or experiences you've had as a result of reading this book I'd love to hear about it. Please send your feedback to:

letterofapology@earthlink.net

If you'd like to contribute an anonymous letter of apology for future editions of the book please send it to:

letterofapology@earthlink.net

Acknowledgements

To all the people who wrote a letter for this book: I want you to know how deeply and profoundly you impacted my writing. Every one of your letters brought tears to my eyes. With the help of your honesty and sincerity I was able to find the words to write the rest of this book. Your letters will help so many people and I am so grateful to you for your courage. Thank you.

To the driver of the SUV: I suppose it's weird to thank someone who caused an accident, but the truth is that if our cars hadn't collided, I wouldn't have met Kathleen and if I hadn't met Kathleen this book might not exist. Thank you.

To Kathleen: There's no doubt in my mind that this book would have been lost if it hadn't been for the opportunity and the encouragement you extended my way. Thank you for both.

To Mary Ellen: For being there. You listened, encouraged and were excited right along with me through the whole process. Thank you.

To Everyone whose eyes sparkled when they heard the idea for this book. Your reactions were a constant inspiration for me to keep working. Thank you.

Letters of Apology

Made in the USA
Charleston, SC
08 September 2012